If Thoughts
Could Kill

I Can Hear what You are
Thinking about Me...

If Thoughts
Could Kill

I Can Hear what You are
Thinking about Me...

Carter M. Head

Heads Up Publications

Atlanta

To: Patricia Morgan
PEACE and Blessing to
You and Your Family

Scripture quotations marked (KJV) are from the King James Version of the Bible.

If Thoughts Could Kill Subtitle: I can Hear what You are Thinking about me…
Copyright © 2020 by Carter M. Head
Published by Heads Up Publications

ISBN: 978-1-7346026-0-9
Ebook ISBN: 978-1-7346026-1-6
Library of Congress Control Number:
2020904442

Heads Up Publications Books are available at special discounts for bulk purchases for sales or premiums.
Direct all inquiries and correspondence to:
Heads Up Publications
P.O Box 162593
Atlanta, GA 30321
e-mail: headsuppublications@gmail.com

Printed in the United States of America

This Book is Dedicated to:

Each of my classmates,
the class of 1982
Jackson High School
Red Devils Butts
County, Georgia.

This Book is in Remembrance of:

Vincent Wise
Wiley Goodman
Kathy Benton
Jeff Butterworth

Robert Mays
Jewel Green
Fred Pope
Jim Pye

Debbie Meredith
Kelly Hardy
Jeff Faulkner
Scott Hall

Brenda Gregory
Bill Powell
Gary Patterson
Jackie Thomas

Contents

Introduction

We all pretend not to be thinking negative about people we connect with on a daily basis when actually we are thinking bad of them and judging them negatively but silently. We have to try and change our bad thoughts about one another. It is possible. This book is written with the hopes of prompting all humans to reconsider our own ways in order to have better mindsets towards one another. This book's motive is to enlighten people to be awakened to the possibility of being able to live in peace in this world no matter what anyone thinks about them from a negative connotation. This compendium will inspire you to be enthusiastic about living with positive thoughts and by not allowing anyone to dictate how you act and feel even when others think negatively about you.

Chapter 1

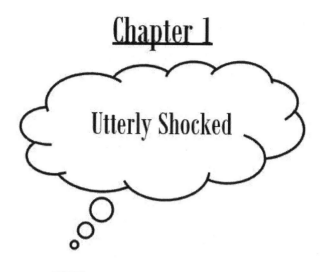

Utterly Shocked

I was inspired to write this compendium late one night after a vivid dream I had. In the dream, there was a familiar face of a known to be a sweet, beautiful and loving lady who expresses her love with just about everyone she meets. She usually hugs and kisses people she relates with, soft-spoken and fun going. But in the dream, I could hear her mind and thoughts towards me, a person who hugs, laughs and converse with me nicely and cordially. I saw and heard her thoughts saying that she and her husband should get me out of their lives and that I was no good and that she did not care for me nor my presence. In which shortly after she expressed those thoughts to me openly. Needless to say, I was shocked.

I was floored with dismay and bewildered surpassed shock. All I wanted to ask was, why did she feel this way about me? I thought we got along well. Our families had a wonderful fellowship going, full of jokes, laughter and sharing good positive information. I just desired from my heart to get an explanation from her on why would she say, think and do this to us and before I could share the encounter with her husband, my friend, I woke up. I Woke up confused, wondering what in the heck that dream meant… So, I began to ponder on and revisit the entire dream and then I had a premonition, but the premonition was not about something bad happening; it was not about this dream actually being true about this lady thoughts and mean actions towards me. It was an inspiration to get up and write about the experience due to the strong feeling that I had. It was something to write and talk about that may be unpleasant to some, but true in essence of facts about we humans and what we think about one another within our secret mindsets, that usually negative thoughts the course of each day.

So I wrote, not only to expose but more to inspire and promulgate self-change in reference to our true hearts and real feelings towards others, especially those close to us in relationships or fellowships.

Chapter 2

Can We be Transparent

What makes God the Creator so unbelievably remarkable and outstanding, to me personally, is God's ability to <u>still</u> love humans even after knowing our thoughts afar off Psalm 139:2 (God knowest our downsitting and our mind uprising, God understandest (perceive) our thoughts afar off. Just imagine if each of us humans could hear the thoughts of one another, especially the minds and thoughts of our associates, friends, coworkers, fellow clergy, fellow parishioners, family members and known enemies. That would not only be an awkward, weird and uncomfortable experience; knowing what each other is thinking, especially in reference to us on a personal level, it would surely be devastating, stressful and confusing to say the least definitely life changing.

I believe an ability like this would cause an uproar like none ever before there would be not only strife, discord, envy and frustration; there would be known hatred towards one another. Well, why such a grave analogy Carter...glad you asked. Because we humans having the gift or ability to read minds would reveal to us on a more drastic and loud level, the facts that most of us really and truly do not like one another, to say it mildly. Secretly most of us hide and camouflage our real thoughts about others, especially the ones close to us. If we could be forced to be totally honest, we humans would admit that all our thoughts, reflections and evaluations of one another are not loving, positive and nice judgments. When we are honest, we humans daily have to oppose the negative critical, judgmental thoughts we think about one another. Let's say only the godly and good people have this warring of the mind going on within our mindsets in reference to you, you and you.

Let's go deeper, surely in this world we all observe and most have experienced the effects of the human discord, by and through the mere fact that we live in a chaotic world full of hatred, lies, deceit, turmoil, racism, division, poverty, murders, premature deaths, man-made disease, financial distress, fighting's, torture, degradation, confusion, abuse, addictions, starvation and wars to name a few. These are some attributes and infractions that are obviously propagated throughout human existence.

On this earth, there's been no known knowledge of documented instances when human opposition never occurred. For example, even in the biblical story of Adam and Eve, their encounter with another form of life brought forth confusion, shamefulness, disobedience, lies and death. Some of you may ask me why write a book like this… my answer is to enlighten some of us humans. I am sure not all, but I am hoping and optimistic that this compendium will reach millions and possibly even billions with my motive being only to bring an awareness of the severity of our human struggles and oppositions towards one another in an effort that most of us would whole heartily at least try to work on our mindsets towards one another. For us all to obtain and experience more peace within ourselves and more peace amongst each other in this world, we live.

It may be farfetched or improbable but think of this idea, as I do; "what if it's even remotely possible for most of us to change how we think about one another to a more loving, empathetic and kinder thoughts, wouldn't that be great." Well, I believe just by having the conversation that presents the idea, you must agree is undoubtedly refreshing to the mind and heart. It will restore hope in humanity.

I remember once, years ago I heard my dad announce on a particular news program on national TV that he had lost his faith and hope in people, he obviously after some 70 years of living in this world had little reasoning to ever believe humanity as a whole would ever get better in operating in and expressing love towards one another consistently. But there was an event, though tragic, prompted my dad to grasp a little hope again that we humans are at least capable of expressing empathy and sharing the love on this earth genuinely. Because in the tragedy, a family of another ethnic group embraced my dad with love and compassion immediately after my dad mistakenly hit their loved one by accident with his car on the expressway. These wonderful people not only embraced my dad with compassion; they continued to express their love towards my dad empathetically, even with gifts and expressions of well wishes. That was many years ago, but periodically they contact me through social media to ask: how my dad is doing. So yes, I am writing this book with the hopes of humbly promulgating us humans to reevaluate our thinking from the negative mindsets we have towards one another, especially amongst those that we know personally, unto the mindsets of being patient, compassionate and empathetic to another. I do believe it is possible with most of us. It just may be a struggle to accomplish it, but we all must at least attempt in an effort to practice having positive thoughts one to another.

I am trusting this book will be a catalyst to begin to subtly prompt us to at least try to think good thoughts about each other on a more consistent level. I am more sure it will not only help ease our minds but would begin the process of healing our relationship with all other people, no matter the ethnicity, creed, color, culture, or religious beliefs. Thank you for considering your ways. What do we have to lose, maybe hatred, murders and even deaths. But think about how our human existence and experiences would be enlightened for the good of all humanity, there would be less wars, little poverty, less murders, we would rarely fight and oppose one another, we would be helpers more towards one another, we would not be judging one another from a negative connotative, but we would see the good first in people. You do realize that God kind of love overrides and pushes away evil most of the time, especially if the one expressing love to another is genuine.

So now, at this point in reading, reflecting, realizing and reconsidering your own ways in which you have been a part of the negative conditions in the world even though on maybe a small aspect. We must admit that there are times, possibly daily, that we as individuals do think negative about one another. The good part about that is, at least some of us override those thoughts and humble ourselves and attempt to allow the love God to flow through us, in spite of the differences, misinterpretations and misunderstandings we sometimes have with each other.

Oh, it's pretty easy for most of us to push back on those bad thoughts we have at times about others, mainly because of the other person's bad actions and character. Still, sometimes we have bad thoughts about other people because of preconceived notions we have in reference to others because we tend to listen to some people that have misinformed us about the very people that we haven't even had the privilege of meeting yet. Please do not allow her, he, nor them to form your opinion about others, especially people you have not even met.

Chapter 3

I Can Hear what You
Think about Me

S o now let's imagine for a few
minutes since we've read
thus far. What if we could
actually hear what others are thinking about
us… Would we be upset, disgusted,
confused, or just sad about how negative
their thoughts were about us? I believe most
of us, if not all, would be surprised at the

negative things people often think about us, especially those people that we perceived loving us and caring about our wellbeing. Just imagine how confusing that would be for you actually to find out, your close companions do not like you and are envious of you, even devising a plan for your demise.

Now, most of us are familiar with and conditioned to others not close to us devising a plan to oppose, kill and destroy us. We see it every day, wars, rumors of wars, fighting, discord amongst different groups, especially in politics and worldly affiliations. We also see the hatred amongst the different ethnicities and cultures and we do see others we do not associate with being territorial; grouping up against each other. But to come to find out through hearing the thoughts of the very people you are in closely connected with, saying loudly without words; that they really secretly hate you or dislike you would be devastating to most of us. Even when we as intelligent humans realize that not all the people we connect with and are close to care that much for us, we still pretend they at least like us a little. We all have a need to be liked, loved, honored, respected and appreciated. So, we go along with the façade of openly expressing fake love and appreciation for each other, especially towards those that have something to offer us because there is usually an underline motive for why people follow and honor us. Like most people, we likewise eventually find out or realize that some are not for us, we then move on without them. But I think it would be a lot different mentally, spiritually and even physically if we all could hear one another negative thoughts towards us, before they show us by their actions, they had disdain for us.

Even though social media and misunderstandings tend to allow us humans to hear, see and realize some people do express openly their dislike, oppositions and disapproval of us, which is sometimes very presumptuous. I think we handle it well most of the time, even though it hurts and bothers us. But again, to have the ability to actually hear or see the person's thoughts about us, especially thoughts that are bad, wrong and degrading would be devasting to many of us. So, I must ask, would you desire to have this gift of reading minds as a part of your everyday psyche? I think not, unless I was more assured that on a average the people that I came in contact with would express mentally a mindset of compassion and empathy towards me, then only would we be excited about utilizing the ability of knowing and seeing what others are thinking. It then would be a wonderful way of communicating without the use of devices. But we must work on the hearts of humans first and express the importance of reconsidering our human tendencies and mindsets, realizing we all could change more for the betterment of all humanity.

Do you have hope that it's possible for people to change inwardly to the point of even our minds showing that we care for one another genuinely? That if and when I can read or hear people's thoughts about me it would be that they esteem me or have respect and admiration towards me. Just think how wonderful that would make us all feel. It would reassure our self-confidence and love for ourselves. It would keep us motivated to do what is right towards each other and it would empower us all to prosper more fervently, living in relaxing peace.

Does this sound like I am dreaming again, or is this wishful thinking. No, I am not dreaming, but it is hopeful thinking, that means it's a possibility for some of us to adhere to this good, positive way of thinking empathetically about everyone. I tell you what, since I wrote this book, I have been choosing to seek ways to operate in love towards all people, especially those that are close associates of mines. At least I've been prompted to try harder and it is actually bringing me more peace, even that peace that surpasses my understandings about others. Why don't you try to see more of the goodness that is in people but not at the expense of it hurting you. Be reminded you can only change your mindset, not the mentality of others. Guard your peace for dear life and allow this book to be one of the instruments and catalyst that inspires many of you to change the way we think about one another. We should be a people that do not continue to judge on our own personal perception of others, because misperception will be the result in most cases.

Chapter 4

Human Thoughts

versus

God's Thoughts

God's love is so Amazing and Inspiring! God's love is definitely unconditional for each of us humans, how I know because The Creator obviously chose not to have destroyed us humans for our thoughts afar off and our negative, hateful, devious mindsets towards one another in this time of our human existence. Do you realize most humans' thoughts are negative? Some neuroscientist studies show a human brain conducts approximately over 6000 thoughts within 24-hours and a significant percentage of those thoughts are negative. God continues to show us all grace and mercy in spite of our wrong and bad behaviors that are usually influenced by our negative thoughts, especially towards other people.

God continues to give us chance after chance. God is giving us all an opportunity to get our mindset together and renewed. It is a choice that we have each day and night to at least consider changing for the better. God is surely not like a human. God do not treat people with cruelty, people treat people with cruelty. People render cruel acts towards one another. God does not respond or react as humans d,o because of a person's negative thoughts in relation to another person. God never thinks as a human think, even the fact God knows all our thoughts good and bad, even our future thoughts about one another. God's ways are past figuring out; such knowledge is too wonderful for us; it is high; we cannot attain unit it. God's greatness is unsearchable (Psalm 139:6).

God's thoughts are nothing like our thoughts, says the Lord. God's ways are far beyond anything we could imagine. So, no human, no matter how much they say they hear from God and God talks to them audibly every day to give them instructions and information about others, do not ever believe it. If people were hearing specifically from God, the Creator they would be doing and thinking way better than humans are usually known to think. I have not ever met a human nor read about a human operating even close to the few ways we understand by biblical scripture to operate. I am not trying to discredit any human, but God said we all are wonderfully made. But we all are flawed in our character and especially our mindsets at times. For those of us that have read the Holy Bible and try to adhere to it as much as possible from of a good heart with positive intentions and with as much love you choose to render towards all others, we even then are lacking in our ability to be able to respect, honor, love and think good about all other humans on a consistent basis. But we can at least do better and decide to do better in our thoughts towards all others by not only reading and applying the idea of trying to think good about people, but we must also practice it. Jesus The Christ, did it according to history and biblical theology. Jesus or Yeshua, a historical figure did walk the earth and did so many great things, which if they were written down in detail, the world itself would not be able to contain the books that would be written (John 21:25).

Again, we humans do not know it all as some of us give the impression that we do, we are just pretending to know God and are pretending to think like God and pretending to operate in the character of God. But what about our thoughts afar off, where do they lead us, are our thoughts evil towards any human? This could possibly be one of the reasons Jesus (Yeshua) sweated in agony and in stress, drops of blood rolled down his face as He prayed. I believe He sweated in agony because he knew the thoughts, ways, actions and the evilness of humans and wanted us be still be redeemed and delivered in spite of. We do have an advocate with God. I do not believe Jesus praying was in vain and of no use. We humans still have a chance to reconsider our evil wicked and selfish ways. We still can choose to change.

We still can decide to at least treat one another better by having and practicing the mindset and heart of compassion, empathy, patience, forgiveness and love. When we begin to operate with the ability to read each other's minds as some scientists say we already can, we just have not tapped into it wholeheartedly; it refers to telepathy. All I know now is that, if we all could read another's minds, at this time would be tragic. We would be angry and traumatized by what we read, especially from the minds of those that we thought loved us for real. But we can start now preparing our hearts to either be ok with or override the negative thoughts others close to have towards us may have. We definitely have a right to work on our own hearts, not thinking evil of no human. It is worth a try, why not, what do you and I have to lose? But we have a lot to gain that is peaceful and good. Remember, the negative things we think and say about others does not solidify who they really are. The essence of a person true identity is up to the individual, not negative comments about them.

Chapter 5

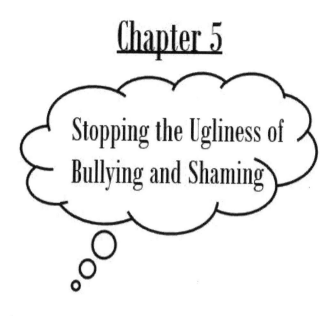

Stopping the Ugliness of Bullying and Shaming

An associate of mines shared with me; that when he and his siblings were younger, they used to love to dance. They would spend time practicing the latest dance moves every day and not to mention they loved to watch the television show Soul Train, which was inspiring to them.

According to him, their parents made them believe they were some of the best dancers they knew, possibly ever. As a result of the inspiring accolades from their parents, this gave him and his siblings the stamina, drive and enthusiasm to practice dancing daily. Also, it encouraged them to be comfortable dancing around other family members and neighborhood friends.

They were confident in the area of their dance skills. Little did they know that when they participated in a middle school dance, their enthusiasm and confidence would be put at a halt even though they knew at the dance their mode could be described as the song: "Getting ' Jiggy Wit It" by Will Smith. The following day after the middle school dance, during recess, a group of kids came up to him and stated,

"you can't dance," he and his siblings asked
the person "how could this be," the leader in
that group said again they couldn't dance,
and they all walked away. Confused, my
associate stated to me how he pondered how
this could be, when they knew they
practiced every day and could dance on beat.
He did not understand how or who to
address this situation with to get clarity of
why a few of these peers would discredit
their skills.

He and his siblings experienced
shame and a taste of loneliness; they went
from dancing every day to eventually
dancing sometimes to being afraid of
dancing in front of people. In middle school,
they did not understand the concept of
people being jealous or having insecurities
to the point some may intentionally say

things to discourage someone else with the motive of diminishing their confidence level. Now, as an adult, they realize if they had shared this shameful incident with their parents, a friend or a school counselor, they would have had an opportunity to look at the situation from a different perspective, instead of being silent and dealing with the negative opinions of others, on their own.

Shame, guilt and being ostracized (excluded from a society or group) to be banished or ignored, can cause some people to be pushed towards the mindset of suicide and to become an introvert. As a result, staying to themselves and their inner thoughts, this can become what I call "Silent Depression," having no outlet and no one to share with. All of us have felt this way at times, we may not have stayed or continued in the mindset of loneliness, but we've all experienced it. But for some, these mindsets of shame, being alone and experienced being bullied and ostracized can become so familiar it forms become our emotional character traits. One of the reasons this happens is because we begin to believe that what others say negative about us is true and as a result of us receiving the negativity from others about ourselves it can weigh us down and destroy us emotionally, causing us to self loathe. Self-loathing unknowingly is a defense mechanism we use in our struggle to be liberated of the painful feelings about our self-worth in which we've suppress our true identities.

Listen, you and I are not who or what they said about us nor thought negatively about us, no matter how many others agreed with their negative analogy of us. We must not allow others, especially those that bully and set out to shame us cause us to react and think negative or depressed about ourselves; this leads to self-hating. We are to practice loving the true essence of who we really are (God's wonderfully made creation). When other people's perception of us prompts us to be ashamed of ourselves, it causes cognitive dissonance in the state of having inconsistent thoughts, beliefs or attitudes about ourselves, especially as relative to behavioral decisions and attitude changes. Again, we must not allow others to dictate how we act, react and feel. There are so many people in this world that do not feel good about themselves because of the negative vibes and negative words coming from others. All of us have experienced this, and you are not alone, you have to choose to override the effects of the damage it caused you. We all must move forward on a quest to be liberated or freed up from the hurts, administered by others.

The national statistics show us that the annual age-adjusted suicide rate is 12.42 per 100,000 individuals. On an average there are 123 suicides per day, my research shows me that many suicides are caused or preempted as an act during a storm of strong emotions and life stresses, dictated by other humans and how they treat us and what we believe they think about us we don't have to be validated by others. We must be extra careful not to develop a need for others to like, love, honor and appreciate us. Because when they don't, it can become frustrating and depressing. Especially when we hear the bad things people say in reference to us. Ninety-four percent of teenage girls have been body shamed and teen boys and men are subjected to thoughtless opinions and hurtful comments made by others as well. Nearly 65% of teen boys reported having been body shamed.

I am so bewildered and bemused or better yet perplexed at the level of hatred and disdain that I recognize throughout this world. My suggestion would be from my heart in reference to my deliverance in the area of me once thinking negative about many people on a consistent basis even at times unknowingly. I was not aware that I was doing it as a norm without any or very little thoughts of conviction. Similar to many of you reading this book who likewise have thoughts about other people that are negative prejudged, unfiltered and unwarranted thoughts that are also condescending and mean spirited. But I have some encouraging news, I as well as so many of us are beginning to be convicted within our hearts of the veracity in the consistency that we have been thinking and talking bad about one another. But also now at this point in our lives, choosing to change for the better of humanity by allowing self-awareness to be illuminated towards the point of reconsidering our ways, with the intensions of looking at others in a good light and thinking more positive in reference to all others, especially of those we have a cordial association with. Those who we choose not to have a friendly relationship with, we move on without the negative connation, we have previously had about them. This is a practice and mindset I have chosen to operate in on this earth amongst my fellow humans as often as I can with a valiant effort each day I live.

   Wouldn't it be awesome camaraderie when more than a few of us reflect consider and apply these concepts of respecting one another and allowing God to love and forgive through us without our resistance... So many people would not have to continue in depression nor have suicidal thoughts. So many would begin on a quest of learning how to love and appreciate the gift of life; God has graced and granted to all of us. Especially those of us reading and adhering to what's written in this compendium. Could this book be a part of the reconditioning of our souls. I say, yes, God uses others to confirm to many of us that we need to change our ways and change starts at us as individuals first.

Chapter 6

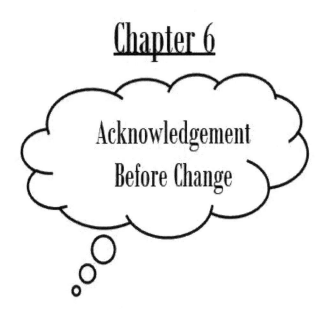

Acknowledgement
Before Change

In order to see, think and react differently, especially on a more positive note. We must first accept or admit the existence or truth of our contentions, flaws and mishaps. There cannot be liberation from wrong doing and negative thoughts towards others, until we all acknowledge we sometimes relate to others with preconceived opinions and ideas.

Which are formed before having the evidence for its truth and validity in reference to people we associate with, people we observe and people we have not meet yet, but someone has shared to us their opinion about them in which we sometimes are prompted to establish our opinion about the ones talked about based on what was shared to us about that person we've never meet. We must be mindful not to listen to the 2nd nor 3rd party information in reference to people we have not meet for ourselves. Those people could possibly be the good connections we need to help us on our great journey towards our positive destiny. Be reminded of my slogan from my book: From Believing to Knowing: That there are 3 sides to every story: his side, her side and then God's side, so always stay neutral.

Biblical scriptures shares and instructs us all, especially believers of God The Creator never to be a partner in nor participate in being a false witness, that speaketh lies, that soweth discord among others and neither have a heart or mindset that deviseth wicked imaginations (Proverbs 6:16-19). We are not to speak evil of others, especially of those we affiliate ourselves with, but we should make or take notice of people who do (Romans 16:17-18 and (James 4:11). We shall lay aside all malice, all guile, hypocrisies, envies and all evil speaking (1 Peter 2:1-25). This is what we should do according to Matthew 5:9; we should practice being peacemakers if we are children of God. Be reminded that gossip or casual, unconstrained conversation and reports about other people, typically involving details that are not confirmed as being true, should cease from each of our lives, whether that be what we think about others negatively, listen to or say.

Gossip negatively hurts and affects people: The gossiper, the listener of the gossip, the person being gossiped about and the people that could have associated with the person gossiped about, but choose not to because of what was stated negatively that was not the truth. This person possibly would have been an asset to the life and advancement of that listener. Gossip also affects the people that are already connected to the person being gossiped about to the point of they also excommunicating themselves from the person being gossiped about, thus prompting a loss of a credible and valuable person being a part of their lives. So, we most definitely need to discover the real concept of changing our mindsets towards all people for the sake of a more positive, productive, loving and peaceful society on this planet.

Chapter 7

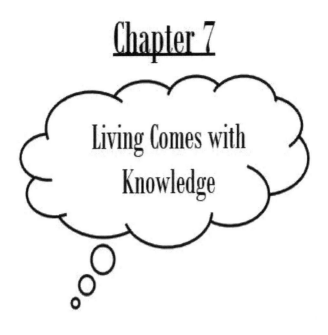

Living Comes with Knowledge

For marital relationships "think for yourself" stop thinking you can change me and what I think. Its time for us all to not only read this book but also apply by only reflecting on our personal way of thinking. This within itself will be difficult, its time for me to fix me first, not my spouse. This chapter will surely prevent divorce, malice, adultery and abuse in most relationships. You will definitely have to read this chapter at least three times in order to receive a full understanding of what I am saying to you, not your spouse or significant other. Remember, change starts with you making a conscious decision to change your negative thoughts in reference to your mate into positive thoughts about them.

Again, you nor I can ever truly sufficiently or thoroughly transform anyone else's negative thoughts. When we try to, the results are usually traumatic, damaging or will lead to a series of breaking up to the point of divorce and even death in some cases. Be careful and be mindful of the negative effects you can have on your mate because of your efforts of trying to change the way he or she thinks about you. I understand your motives is to get you both on the same page, at least, you know, as a power team, always in agreement, living happier ever after. Listen, that's by far wishful thinking, to say the least. But I have discovered a sure-fire way to alleviate the distresses of marriage and relationships. Again, read this chapter three times with an open mind and with a heart for positive change in your relationship. Here's how: with harmony and according to what you know and have to come to realize throughout the relationship.

Have you ever took notice of these facts about your significant other; no matter how much you accomplish in status, finances, material things and yes even intimately, the enthusiasm and happiness of the rewarding experiences, seems to always, throughout your relationship, be brief or short in time period, at least until the next great experience. The joy and appreciation never seem to last on a consistent or lengthy period, and this bothers us, thus prompting our negative thoughts towards one another in our relationship. I understand this is very discouraging at times and this lack of consistency of showing appreciation can give pause to some negative thoughts and some thoughts of the "grass is greener on the other field" in other words, some us start thinking how good it would be sharing time with any person who would possibly appreciated us more. Now do I have your attention? Look around and make sure your spouse is not watching you read this chapter because this book is talking to you! On a personal level. So, I must inform you: your thoughts about your significant others will not change them!

If you continue to express your thoughts about them doing better openly, it will only make the relationship stressful and taxing on your mind, body and the end results will be possibly death in some cases. Let's all calm, reevaluate our own ways and how we have been mishandling our relationships. By first changing the way we think about the one we supposed to love and enjoy life with as teammates and lovers. Again, by now, you do realize that it is unproductive and usually futile in the way you been handling the situation. Let's try another approach; do not expect him or her to be happy on a consistent level every day. It will not happen. <u>Acknowledging</u> that obvious fact will begin the process of you walking in more peace in your house. We must also <u>acknowledge</u> within our mindsets that they are not us and their thoughts and ways will never be the same as your thoughts are because you are unique, and they have a God-given right to their true identity and thoughts as well.

So, we must respect one another's personal perspectives and way of thinking, remembering you arguing and opposing their way of thinking will not change them. You are wasting your time and are contributing to the distress and turmoil in your relationship and this results in unhappiness, divorce, cheating, lying, and fighting. Let's go deeper: by acknowledging or realizing what provokes misunderstandings and anger, we can then choose to live better. Not under a false pretense: that if we keep trying to change them the way we desire them to be will fix the problem, it will not. We have to respect their God-given right to think with their intellectual reasoning. We must only control our own thoughts and if our thoughts are not thoughts of peace, forgiveness, love, joy, giving and harmony, we need to practice operating in our relationships with these thoughts, even when our spouse or significant other is not and will not because both of us in the relationship can't continue to contribute to the demise of the fellowship. So after <u>acknowledging</u> its not like their responsibility to change but yours. You can then get your focus off what they are doing wrong and put the focus on yourself. Knowing the other person's focus should be on changing their own thoughts for the betterment of the relationship.

Remember, though you are together, you both have different purposes on this earth and obviously, in the union, acknowledge that daily within your thoughts. Because; warning! Warning! When you focus too much on them, you will not be able to change your perception and way of thinking in reference to the relationship on a more positive perspective. Negative thinking fuel thoughts of jealousy, envy, strife and especially delusions. Sometimes in order to get past these issues we must as an individual overlook these positions and thoughts and refocus on ourselves, not allowing our own thoughts to go there as well. I am optimistic that you both can become a team paying, power couple. But it starts with you, not them. You may not be on the same page, but I pray you both are at least in the same book. This means your relationship has a chance. Now hold on that wasn't a question. So why are you saying in your thoughts, "my significant other is not even in the same book." Look maybe not, but after we get your mindset change, it's a possibility you both will be, not only in the same book but eventually on the same page living with one another according to acknowledge. Now, are you finally getting it? Well, receive it by applying what this book is sharing.

Again, her assignments and ways are hers. His assignments and ways of thinking are his. Do not try to make her or him equal with your ways. By respecting them as being different than you. Its okay as long as you believe and know you both are wonderfully made by our God The Creator. I guess God has a sense of humor when He made me and you because we all are a work undone, we are not quite finished yet. My prayer is for both and all of us humans, to consider thinking better about one another. Finally, first Peter chapter 2 verse 1 and verse 7 instructs us both (he and her) to live (means to have abundant fulfilled living) with our spouses according to knowledge (what we realize about them on their individual level, not overriding and not changing their level, but adhering to, respecting and honoring where they are at mentally and intellectually right now, without being disrespectful but relating to them accordingly in harmony).

Let's try this approach. Peace and blessing upon you both.

Chapter 8

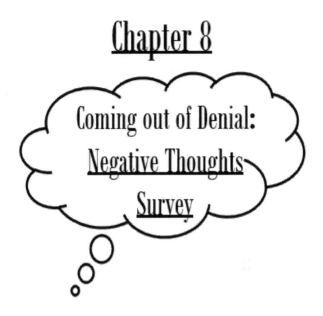

Coming out of Denial: Negative Thoughts Survey

If you have silently thought or said out loud any 5 of these thoughts, please reread this book again...

Be reminded, though most of these thoughts and sayings may be true attributes of many people we come in contact with. Let's look at it from this perspective; if we can spend effort, energy, perception and time to think and say negative things about each other, why not use that same effort and observation to try and produce good positive thoughts and sayings about others.

Here are some things we think and say in reference to one another:

Which ones have you thought or said?

Let's put these saying in categories.

Religious

1. They are not really saved for real
2. They know that's too tight
3. They can't sing
4. They are shacking
5. They preach too long
6. They didn't have to say that
7. They think they are something
8. They are too fat
9. Look at them
10. They don't have no Holy Ghost

11. They are always late

12. They are ugly

13. That outfit is ugly

14. They need to sit down

15. Lost

Jobs/Careers

1. They always kiss up

2. They are nothing but a snitch

3. They are always late

4. They are lazy

5. They smell

6. Who do they think they are

7. They never will get it

8. They are noting but gossipers

9. They micromanage

10. They are a real bad boss

11. I don't like working with them

12. I don't trust them

13. They get on my nerve

School/Classes

1. They are cheating
2. They think they are smart
3. They are just dumb
4. They are fat
5. Their clothes are raggedy
6. They are too short
7. They are ugly
8. They are the teacher's pet
9. Look at them
10. I hate them
11. They are stupid
12. They are too skinny
13. Look their ugly hair
14. That teacher is crazy
15. You are not my mother/father

Out in the public

1. Look at their prejudice self
2. Look at their plate, it's too much

3. They are too fat

4. They are just ugly

5. They need to pull those pants up

6. Look at the Bitch

7. Look at them bad kids

8. They are racist

9. Hillbillies

10. Nigger

11. I hate them

12. Cracker

13. Stupid

14. Dumb ass

15. Devils

16. Poor

17. Trash

Family

1. They are selfless

2. They are stupid

3. They never participate

4. I am the black sheep

5. They are too mean

6. They are dope addicts

7. They are alcoholics

8. They never give/never help no one

9. They just like their dad

10. They know they shouldn't wear that

11. They are always broke

12. They need to fix their hair

13. What do they want now

14. They don't get along

15. They don't even care

16. They abused me

17. They raped me

18. All he did was cheat

19. He/she no good

20. She acts like she's the mom

21. He's too weak

22. All they do is fight

23. She/he needs to leave him/her

24. Look at them bad kids

25. I can't stand them

Political arena

1. They are communist

2. They are race baiters

3. They are leftist

4. They are far right

5. They are bad immigrants

6. Racist

7. Out of touch

8. Communists

It is absolutely mind-blowing how so easily and nonchalantly we can think negative and say bad things about others, its like second nature. Ephesians 4:29 instructs us not to allow corrupt communication to proceed out of our mouth; we should be edifying or building up others. 1 Corinthians 15:33, Evil company corrupts good habits. Be careful, who you are listening to and choose to start practicing thinking good and pleasant things about others, it takes stressing away and it promotes peace amongst us.

Please do not allow your thoughts to kill, destroy, denigrate and belittle others, not even if the negative perceptions are facts. Be reminded; blessings and cursing's should not come out of the same mouth. Speak life and live longer in peace. Please reconsider your ways. Know and realize that just because you say it or think bad about people, does not solidify who they and we really are. The essence of our true identity is what actually matters. Who we are is not predicated on what anyone else says or think about us.

May the peace of God rule and override any negative thought you may ever have about yourself or that others have in reference to you. I love you and honor you. I am so happy to know that since you read this book, what others think about you negatively will not kill you anymore!

Other Books by the Author

◊ Lying Mirrors

◊ Unity for What?

◊ Am I Trump?

◊ From Believing to Knowing

◊ Questions with no Answers

About the Author

Carter M. Head is a life coach, a minister, and is one of the most dynamic, realistic, and sought-out conference speakers. Carter is a graduate of Andersonville Theological Seminary and Alumni of West Georgia College. Carter founded and established many outreach organizations in reference to feeding and clothing the indigent. Carter also established the YL2 (Youth Leadership League of Henry County, GA), and he coproduced three live stage plays emphasizing on the issues of our youth. Carter established the mentoring group called B.I.N.O. In addition, Carter is an author, grant writer, marriage counselor, and philanthropist.

Direct all inquiries and correspondence to:

Heads Up Publications
c/o Carter M. Head
P.O Box 162593
Atlanta, GA 30321

Made in USA - Crawfordsville, IN
38086_9781734602609
04.27.2020 0952